INSPIRATIONS

All inquiries should be addressed to:

Book Domain LLC.
543 E Louise Dr Phoenix, Az 85050

Ordering Information:

Amount Deals. Special rebates are accessible on the amount bought by corporations, associations, and others. For points of interest, contact the distributor at the address above.

Printed in the United States of America.

ISBN-13   Paperback   978-1-967903-67-2
          eBook   978-1-967903-66-5

INSPIRATIONS

DENSON JONES

CONTENTS

When everything is going right, something will sometimes go wrong.

As a Navy Veteran, I was taught about Honor, Respect, and Dignity. To know and Tell the Truth is the Essence of All humans. I write these Quotes for those who seek the Truth who Loves Justice and Believes in the Ethics of Life. I am inspired to write from listening to everyday people, from Facebook, Movies, even Instant Messaging.

I am just inspired by Everyday life. I hope and pray that the readers of these Quotes Believe and Enjoy a part of what I believe in from my life's Experience's. May The Dream Merchant, at some point in time, make Most of your Dreams Come True.

When everything is going right, something will sometimes go wrong. I am dedicating this book to my parents Mr. Denson Joe Jones and Mrs. Barbara Ann Jones.

INSPIRATIONS

S. Navy Camp Berry
"Boot Camp"

1. A good man is never hard to find, but he might be hard to keep.

2. Fool me once, shame on you. Fool me twice, shame on you again.

3. In order for you to see the light, you have to come out of the dark.

4. Never raise me up. to let me down.

5. After all the wonders and beauty that you have seen in this world, plus the miracles of birth, if you still don't believe in God, then you are truly a lost soul.

6. Bad things happen to good people so they can further have faith in the Lord to help them.

7. If you only see a little, you will never see the whole.

8. If you put up with it, you'll end up with it.

9. I am not good as I want to be, but I am better than I used to be.

10. If you are not ambitious about a thing, you are not going to be a success about a thing.

11. Live for something, don't die for nothing.

12. Although you don't see me, and you still trust in me, that is what I call faith.

13. God is in everyone, but everyone is not in God.

14. The truth will always follow you. It may never catch you, but Karma will.

15. You may slow me down, but you will not stop me.

16. The best team doesn't always win; but the team that plays the best sometimes will.

17. If at first you don't succeed, wait for another day and try, try again. Don't ever give up.

18. If I can touch it, I can catch it.

19. You can never win if you beat yourself.

20. I do unto you, as you do unto me.

21. Step back and let us go thru, because here we come, and here we go.

22. Don't ever give it all away, keep some for yourself.

23. The day u stop laughing is the day u start to die inside.

24. We all should have common sense, but some do not choose to use it.

25. If God does not Change, his Doctrine does not Change.

26. If you gamble with the future, you might forget the past.

27. I gave it to you the first time, and if you didn't succeed the second time; you had the chance and that is, the possibility of future success.

28. Stop talking about it, and quit thinking about it, just do it.

29. If you take care of me, I will take care of you.

30. If you have a strategy about life be committed and forceful.

31. You can play the game the best that you can, but you can never win by yourself.

32. You might be thru with the past, but the past may not be thru with you.

33. Sometimes you go in as the challenger, but you come out as the champ.

34. Sometimes helping others that are less fortunate feels better than helping thyself.

35. Sometimes we don't want to just make things easier, we want to sweeten the bitter.

36. Money, might not be able to buy you love, but, it sure can buy you happiness.

37. If we All are aware of the content of a person's character. And respect that. We should be able to get along. Peace and Respect is the Key.

38. If you don't have something to die for, what do you have to live for?

39. Depression can rarely catch up with a person with a fast mind.

40. Sometime you have to adlib life, because you can't plan everything.

41. Many a truth is spoken jokingly.

42. Some people hate for no reason at all. Just for the sake of hating.

43. Black folks are like the Sun, you can cover us from shining for a moment in time, but we are still there and we aren't going anywhere.

44. I'll be there in a skinnet, and that's quicker than a minute.

45. I am who I am, because of who I am.

46. If you go for the norm, you will never be special.

47. When you stop thriving, you stop achieving.

48. I am not a cracker, I am a care giver because I give care, I don't take it.

49. The only thing Greater than thyself is thy smaller self.

50. If right is right, you can't make it wrong. If wrong is wrong, you can't make it right.

51. We should, Live, Love, and Laugh every day.

52. We should Love, Laugh, and Live every day.

53. You matter to somebody, so you matter to me.

54. In my book, Quality beats Quantity Every time.

55. No matter how far you go forward, you will always look back.

56. When you have a chance to dance, you should just dance.

57. Don't change so people will like the fake you. Be yourself & the right people will love the real you.

58. If you shoot for the moon and land on a star, that is good enough for me.

59. You take what you can get, until you can get what you want.

60. Remember that, a Nobody is Still Somebody to Somebody.

61. There is no greater love than Brotherly love, because you choose to love a stranger.

62. If you give freely, you will get freely.

63. If you are right, you can never be wrong.

64. Where can you do the most good, without doing yourself harm?

65. Tomorrow is Always a new day.

66. When you stand to win, you have to understand that you can lose too.

67. To have life is to live, so live your life.

68. Sometimes God lets good things fall apart, so bad things can fall together.

69. Ambition, Willpower, and Determination is what we all need to succeed.

70. If you give with all your heart, it's not about how much you give; it's about the love you put into giving.

71. Sometimes doing the right thing is not easy.

72. When the bad comes looking for you, and it will, keep you r head down and let it pass you by.

73. Starting is just the beginning, but it's worth it, when you get to the end.

74. The best relationship that you can have in this world is with our Lord.

75. There is One that is Always Greater than thy self and that is our God.

76. When you argue with a fool, what does that make you?

77. When Evil comes to your front door, let it out your back door.

78. Look out for Evil, because sometimes, it will follow you home.

79. Never give up, for that is the time when things change for the worse.

80. Don't ever cry about the spill milk, because daddy is around the corner with a whole bucket full.

81. When you look in the mirror and see evil, stop looking in that mirror.

82. Sometime it's okay to disturb the sounds of silence.

83. At one time, if you are younger than me. I was your age before you were your age.

84. You should look at Everything as a Lesson.

85. If you don't know where you come form, you won't have a dream of where you're going.

86. Sometimes, you don't know how you are going to do it, or when you are going to do it. You just know that you have to do it.

87. Sometimes I think about the worse, until I see the best.

88. What you do at the beginning, will affect you at the end.

89. Sometimes it takes little parts to make a whole.

90. I used to say in football practice, if I can touch it, I can catch it.

91. The boy I was yesteryear is not the man I became.

92. Never give it up today, you will give up tomorrow.

93. If you give up today, you will give up tomorrow.

94. If age is nothing but a number, why is that number always changing?

95. If loving you is wrong, then I will be wrong forever

96. When you believe in a vision you don't see, that is called faith.

97. If you keep going back to the past, you must want to go live there.

98. In the End, the Good always beats the Evil.

99. Always do the most good, without doing the most harm.

100. Sometimes the hard way could be the only way.

101. If you ever find your True Destiny, look for someone to share it with, don't do it alone because with someone else it could mean love.

INSPIRATIONS

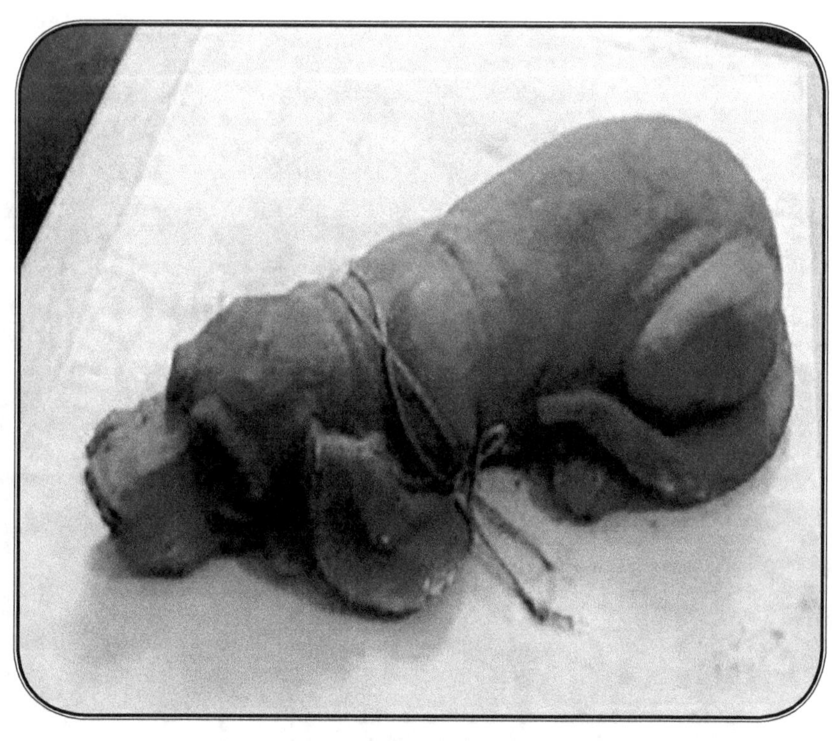

*Do what a clock does; keep on ticking and
moving toward something.*

1. If you take my Eye, I will take your Tooth.

2. When the Truth is told, the Wicked flees.

3. Some times when things happen, it's just the way things works out.

4. O live Serendipity, because it is something that happens again for a reason.

5. You Worship the Lord on the Seventh Day, You Praise him Every Day.

6. Sometime you meet your destiny on the road that you try to avoid.

7. If you don't fake it, you might be able to make it.

8. Sometimes slow and easy wins the race. A slow progress is still progress.

9. It is hard sometimes for the brain to process the truth.

10. When we lose a loved one the pain slowly heals and we find a way to fill the void left in our hearts.

11. Sometimes it hurts so bad, but it feels so good.

12. When you get pushed hard from a mentor, it's to get you ready.

13. If you learn from yesterday, live for today, and hope for tomorrow, you should remember to never stop learning.

14. Your vision will become clear when you look into your heart, mind and soul.

15. The old will never catch up to the new.

16. It's not how big your body is, but how big your heart is.

17. Even if you come out of hell on fire, you came out.

18. We all can overcome our fears by the action that we do.

19. Nature accomplishes the whole universe, because she never rushes.

20. Sometimes life gives you nothing. And other times it hits you all at once.

21. Sometimes when you want to go, it's time for you to go.

22. To be happy or sad, takes the same amount of work.

23. If you can dream it, you can do it.

24. If you can't expect the truth from someone, don't expect loyalty.

25. You can be anti-social with the social world, but be social with the real one.

26. We as humans have different nationalities, but we all are the same.

27. When we make bad choices, we have to live with them.

28. If you don't learn from your past, you might repeat it in the future.

29. Sometimes the answer to our questions can be found in the past.

30. Sometimes we must scratch the surface to see what lies beneath.

31. Sometimes the best way to leave an impression is to just leave.

32. I know a thing or two, because I've experienced a thing or two.

33. If it wasn't for pressure, we wouldn't have diamonds.

34. When you earn something, you deserve something.

35. When we focus on things above, the Lord has our backs, if we believe.

36. Sometimes we do things to punctuate our boredom.

37. When life speaks, you better listen.

38. Always remember your vision is your focus. Without it, you cannot see.

39. Sometimes we may have to fight, remember to fight the good fight.

40. If you ever really want Salvation, just open the door and let Jesus in.

41. Our lives will never be perfect but you just have to keep working on it.

42. Your destination should be a beautiful journey.

43. When you think about it, it's the life in our years that really matter.

44. When you take a picture, I see things thru your eyes.

45. If you want to win the race, you have to keep moving forward.

46. If the cause is credible, I'd die on my feet, instead of living on my knees.

47. Sometimes, the people that love us the most know us better than we know ourselves.

48. We should have faith in the word of God, not necessarily in who brings it.

49. Confidence and Fauth should never go out of style.

50. If you have the courage to tell it, you should have the courage to live it.

51. Trust is a tough thing to have in any relationship, but you have to have it to make your relationship last.

52. We all have the potential of greatness within us.

53. Live for something and die for something.

54. Sometimes we play for money, and sometimes for respect.

55. Before you ask others for help, you need to learn to help yourself.

56. If you can dream it you can be it.

57. Sometimes what we leave behind catches up with us.

58. If I can pay the price for being wrong, can you pay the price for me being right?

59. There are Bad Reasons, Good Reasons, and Real Reasons.

60. If you compete with no one, no one can compete with you.

61. You have to have your Spirit right to be able to laugh.

62. With persistence, we all can see our dreams come true.

63. How many eyes have seen their dreams come true?

64. You can tell an actor by the way they act.

65. The door swings both ways when a man or woman demand loyalty and respect.

66. Minimum risk could lead to Minimum Profit.

67. Sometimes it's not about Love, it's about Trust.

68. Sometimes it's not about Trust, it's about Love.

69. If we can do it, we Teach it.

70. You should make sure you use the right parameters for success.

71. To forgive someone that betrayed you is doable. To trust them is optional.

72. To be a success, we all have to conquer the highest plateau.

73. Everything that we get we should earn.

74. A job worth doing is worth doing right the first time.

75. If you can't accept the fact that certain things will never be the same as they used to be, then you are delusional.

76. You might be one person, but you have to the person that matters most.

77. You are a Target, because you are a Threat.

78. Your final destination should not be your current situation.

79. Faith is when you don't see a way but God makes a way.

80. You shouldn't steal it, you should earn it.

81. Sometimes what we pretend to be we become.

82. You should always have at least one person around you in your life that you can be you.

83. In ten or twenty years from now, if you regret not doing the things you haven't done versus the things that you have done, then start doing them.

84. Our environment can make us bad, but we are taught to be good.

85. Before we die, we all should live our lives freely and comfortably.

86. When it comes to right and wrong, we have to choose which side to be on.

87. It's nothing quite like the sound of laughter.

88. If no one wants you when you're down and out, then try to stay up.

89. If God wanted humans to fly, he would have made us Angels with wings.

90. One thing that human beings are consistently good at is killing. We need more Peace.

91. If trouble ever comes to my door let me take the brunt of it so my children may not suffer.

92. I may not know what I'm going to get out of life, but I know what I need.

93. You are my Sunshine and my Life. My existence revolves around you very Being.

94. When you argue with a fool, a fool comes out of you.

95. If you ever question if you are strong enough to make it, do what you have to do to strengthen your core and your Soul.

96. We should All be like the Cream of the Crop, Always rising to the Top.

97. If you ever want to be a pilot, you first have to get on the plane.

98. I'm never going to stop till my cup runneth over.

99. If you live with the thought that anything can happen, then you can be ready for it to happen, good or bad.

100. If you are all that you can be that is good enough.

3

INSPIRATIONS

*You will have a lot of ups and downs in life
but you just have to ride it out.*

1. The Day you Stop Dreaming, That's the Day you Start Dying.

2. You can't pay your bills with other people's opinions.

3. All of us need support, especially when we are wrong.

4. When distance and time can't break you apart, you are connected Heart to Heart.

5. Never put your Dreams on hold so your children can realize theirs maintain your Dreams first then adhere to your children's.

6. The Greatest loss in Life is to not believe in Jesus.

7. Everything has its place in the Circle of Life.

8. Sometimes the dirt on you will never wash off.

9. Medications inhibit our illusions, not our fantasies.

10. Live your life until it's over.

11. We don't need to be Financially Rich; we just need to Spiritually Rich.

12. When God sends food and the Devil sends cooks, don't eat the Devil's cooking.

13. Keep your Soul in high spirits because a sad Soul can kill.

14. We run away from our roots to start new roots. But we should always return to see where we started from.

15. It would be so embarrassing if you are trying to keep up with the Jone's but can't, and you Are a Jones.

16. Sometimes you can't just say it, you have to do it.

17. If they do it like that you have to do it like this. If they do it like this you have to do it like that.

18. If you are not ready to clean your house up, you shouldn't have a house.

19. If your church keeps secret Sins, it's time to get a new church.

20. Everywhere there is a pocket of darkness, the Lord thy God will bring to the Light.

21. If the Devil finds work for idle hands, then stay busy.

22. Can a Heart be healed without daring to believe?

23. When you dance with the Devil, you will stay in Hell.

24. If you are failing at something it could mean you need to learn how to struggle.

25. You have to be there to Really Understand.

26. If you want to walk in a man's shoes, you must be ready to wear some pretty Big Shoes.

27. The only way to let the Devil in your house is you have to let him in.

28. You might be able to scam some of the people of the time, but you can't scam All of the people All of the time.

29. You will always be right, when you do good.

30. I don't need a lot of materialistic things in my life; I just want to live Happy and Comfortable.

31. Remember when you make a promise to God; the Devil knows how to also.

32. Anytime you get to the end of one thing, look for the beginning of another thing.

33. Until you give them life, Opinions are just Opinions.

34. If common sense doesn't come with a degree, then get a degree

35. You might be a broken crayon, but you still color the same.

36. If you are a limited edition, that means there are less copies.

37. You can never change a Lie to equal the Truth.

38. In Heaven, we will see the High brought Low.

39. Sometimes you have to follow your Demons and sometimes your Demons follow you.

40. Anything you have to change cannot be an Original.

41. No matter how big you get in this life, your grave will be the same size as mine.

42. All dreams aren't meant to come true, some should just remain dreams.

43. If misery loves company don't have so much company.

44. If it only takes a moment to make a moment, then make it your business to make that moment.

45. Some people think that just because you earned it, you don't deserve it. I beg to differ.

46. Have you ever pinched yourself while you were dreaming? Me neither.

47. Sometimes a lie has to die, before the truth can live.

48. We all were born to Live, so let's Live.

49. If you learned any lesson from personal experience, pass it forward.

50. Our parents are like fruit trees. When we are born, They give us all of their fruits for food, and one day we grow up and leave. Then we come back because we need shelter, They give us their branches. Then we come back again and want to play, so They give us their trunk. We come back again and want to rest because we are older now and our parents say lay on my loots. So no matter what, our parents will do everything They can just to keep us happy and keep Their Forest Growing.

51. It is Easy to Take away Your Rights if You Don't even Know Them.

52. You can't live your life Backwards, So Live It Forwards.

53. Sometimes in order to go forward, you have to look backwards.

54. Sometimes we have to fail, so we can learn how to Win.

55. Sometimes we cross certain lines and can never go back.

56. Every team plans and plays to Win.

57. When we open someone's personal door, we open up their life.

58. He said that he could do it, and he Really Believed that he could do it, so he did it.

59. Sometimes we all need to just Believe.

60. If you want to serve and protect, you can't be scared or fear for your life. Don't use this as an excuse to kill.

61. You might call me a dreamer but I want to see a world where all the races of humans can live as one.

62. We might come from different streets but we can still have the same dreams.

63. If u can see in, I could see out.

64. Sometimes what our enemies do to us, we do to ourselves.

65. Be like a butterfly and fly as high as you can.

66. In today's world' justice isn't won in the courtroom.

67. A partner is made to have your back.

68. All cops should learn about the citizens in the communities that they protect and serve.

69. You are a fool if you are led by a fool.

70. If We live without Honor, We must Die without Honor.

71. If you love me, do not doubt me.

72. If you talk in the Single Vernacular, you can't use And.

73. Faith is when you don't understand, but you Still believe.

74. When you are in a dark place a True Friend will bring you to the light.

75. Some people say they thought they had seen it All. I say, it is always more to come. So you will never see it All.

76. If They Treat you like Somebody instead of Nobody, Keep Them.

77. If you do it, that just shows it could and can be done.

78. When you speak for the Truth, you gave to Fight for the Truth.

79. A Beacon is a Light used to give us Hope.

80. You don't have to be a star to be in My show.

81. You can never steal memory.

82. All progress lost has to start all over again.

83. Our Evil works shall become Null and Void.

84. If you don't appreciate it now just lose it tomorrow and see how you feel when it's gone.

85. Sometimes some of us are just trying to sell the Truth.

86. They say money can't buy you happiness, wo what can being broke buy you?

87. Once I give you my Prescription, I want to see it Filled.

88. No one knows the Structure of a building, better than the Architect.

89. Everything comes to an End.

90. When things go wrong with us, we talk to a Psychiatrist for help. So when things go wrong with Them, Who do they talk to or go to for help?

91. When Talking about The Past, We All are Deprived of Something that Might have been.

92. The Bad thing about following Man's Doctrine in being Religious is that They Teach You to Believe that You can start Over Every week.

93. If you Watch people do Evil and do nothing, what does that make You?

94. If you Learn to Get Love, You have to Learn how to Give Love.

95. When we let go of our Past, our Future looks Brighter.

96. If you believe in Fairytales, let me be your Knight.

97. You should close one door before you open another one.

98. Rehabilitation is just like Prayer, it Works.

99. If I don't let you Reach Me, you will Never bring me Down.

100. Apologize for being Wrong, but Never for being Right.

INSPIRATIONS

The Mother of my first daughter and my daughter together

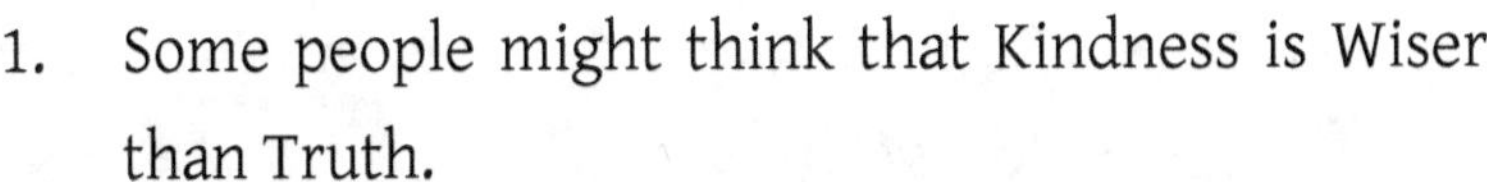

1. Some people might think that Kindness is Wiser than Truth.

2. No matter how Low you go, I will always be there for you.

3. If you hate someone for Correcting You, You're a Fool.

4. If you are hired to Serve and Protect and You Fear for Your life, don't serve.

5. Real Heros don't use Excuses to fight for Justice and Liberty.

6. I know What to DO When it's Time to Do What it is to Do.

7. When I Need It, I Do It.

8. I'd rather live Happy Without you, that Sad Living Beside you.

9. When Life gives a Wakeup call, You Better Answer.

10. A Hypocrite, is jus another name for Bad Manners.

11. Sometimes the Truth can kill. But some people aren't Afraid to Speak it.

12. If you want things to Change, You have to Change Them.

13. When we tell the Truth, we Shame the Devil.

14. Don't appreciate your loved ones when it's too late for them to appreciate your Appreciation.

15. Your Children Will Never be Older than You.

16. Money is like Your Life. How are You going to spend Yours?

17. If you play with fire and Never Learn, you will get Burned.

18. Pain Teaches us All a Lesson.

19. Sometimes when we Don't Think about it, we Won't Do it.

20. A Hero is someone who displays Grace and Bravery under Pressure.

21. When you talk bad about someone, you Also are also talking about Yourself.

22. Sometimes Great Events are Often Decided by Pure Chance.

23. If a Picture is worth a Thousand words, a Thousand words should be worth a Picture.

24. The Best team doesn't Always Win. But the team that plays the Best time Usually Does.

25. If I die for you, You have to Survive for Me.

26. When you tell the Truth to Shame the Devil, You Might make the Lord Smile.

27. Follow the Lord thy God, and You shall be Free.

28. Never write a check with your Mouth that your Body Can't Cash.

29. You should Know the Future if you help Build it.

30. What's the sense of having Cake when you can't eat it?

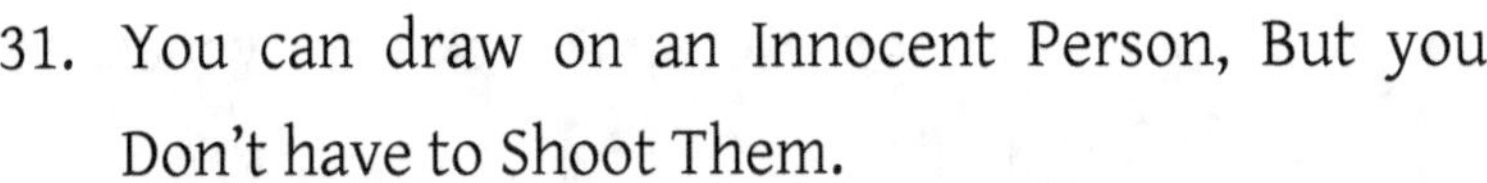

31. You can draw on an Innocent Person, But you Don't have to Shoot Them.

32. Before you find out Who Someone else is and Where They Came from, find out Who You are and Where You Came from.

33. Give what you can When you can.

34. You will Always Miss the Things that you Think you Won't.

35. Injuries will heal, but a Nasty Rumer never dies.

36. Don't Ever put your Pride before your Life.

37. We Thank God for All the Good things that happen to us, Yet Blame him for All the Bad.

38. If you would give your Life for Jesus, you have to Also give your Soul.

39. Do people know what you are Talking about, when you are Talking about what you are Talking about?

40. The Quality should Always go in, Before the Name goes on.

41. When Your Mind is Blind, What use are your Eyes?

42. If You Can't Stop, Then Don't Stop.

43. If God Opens a door for you, No man can Ever Shut it.

44. Every Personality Has a Story and a Character.

45. If hair is the Glory of a Woman, Why then do you Cut it Short?

46. Sometimes Choice and Luck Intervenes. What's your Opinion?

47. If I Whisper You the Truth, Will You Still Hear me?

48. I don't want you to just Die for me, Survive for me.

49. If you lay down Your Life for Me, Will You Then be Free?

50. A Lie Can Change Many times, But the Truth Never Changes.

51. If All of your life, you are Trained to Follow Man's Doctrine, Stop. Now and Follow the Ways of the Lord Thy God.

52. If You Will be Honest and True, Karma Will Always come Back to you.

53. You can make as many Wrong decisions as possible, but Our Lord in Heaven Still Loves You.

54. When you do Right, you Never have to Fear for Anything.

55. Don't worry about making a Living. Worry about making Your Life worth Living.

56. It's better to go out as a Zero, and make it to Heaven, Than go out as a Hero and go to Hell's fire.

57. You can Learn a Lot if you just sit back, Listen and Observe.

58. Sometimes good enough is Really Not Good Enough.

59. If You Don't Do Anything about it, Don't Say Anything about it.

60. We Don't Trust Everybody because Everybody Can't be Trusted.

61. If it feels Right, Just Do it.

62. The Thing about a Double Standard is, You get away with Everything, and I don't.

63. You Can't hold hands with God, and Run with the Devil.

64. No matter what we do in this world, It Just keeps Turning.

65. We All Should do two things every day, Laugh and Love.

66. The Devil's Plan is to let us Blame Our Lord for Disasters, But We Still have to Live by Faith in His Word.

67. If you Fail to Plan, You Might Just be Planning to Fail.

68. I Believe that people Cling to Hatred Because, Once it's Gone, They will be forced to Face the Pain of Truth.

69. To Reach the Unreachable Star, You Just have to Reach.

70. Live to Forgive, Love and Learn.

71. To Start you have to begin, To Begin you have to Start.

72. What we do Today, will Certainly Affect Tomorrow.

73. Even If we take on step forward and you knock us One Hundred steps back, We Will just Keep on Stepping Forward.

74. When we Eliminate the Impossible, We Must Recognize the Truth.

75. When you plan to work, you work to plan.

76. Sometimes it is Good to Visit, But Not Too Good to Stay.

77. If you have to Wait for Tomorrow, you must not be Able Today.

78. If you Live Life, Live it the Right Way.

79. Thanks for teaching me what I need to Learn.

80. If We Change our Perspectives, We have to Change Period.

81. You should do the Right Thing for the Right Reasons.

82. If you refuse to see Evil that lives with you, Don't be surprised if it completely Destroys you.

83. If you have a Voice, let it be Heard.

84. As a Navy Veteran I never died for my country, But I Will die for my Family. When I Speak, I want you to Lsiten. And when you are Ready to Listen, I will Speak.

85. When you get caught in a Lie, and you continue to lie, you are a Habitual Lier.

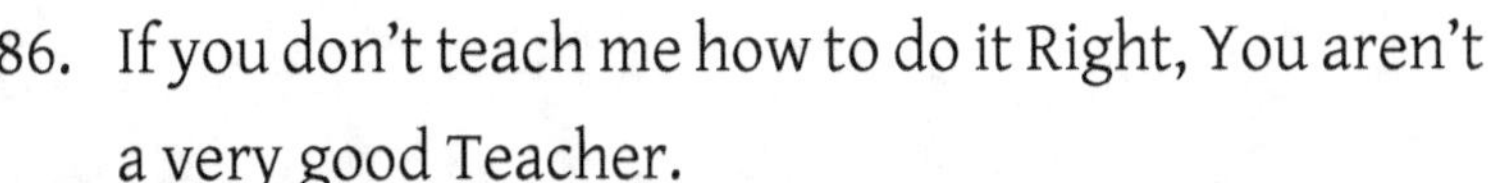

86. If you don't teach me how to do it Right, You aren't a very good Teacher.

87. When you see Sinners, should you and would you give Them Love?

88. One Thing that Can Not be Taken Away form our Lord Thy God, is his Name.

89. We should All Stand against Evil Doers.

90. I do what I do because I am who I am.

91. Is it Not Our Place to Ask Why Things happen?

92. Can you come back at Me, when I am coming back at You?

93. How can we go Back to a Place that we have Never Been?

94. If you see something bad, you should Always Say Something.

95. You can't hold hands with the Lord and Walk with the Devil.

96. If you can't remember your Lie, the Devil might be in the Details.

97. If You Just Learn Who I am, You Just Might Like Me.

98. What is a Shadow? A figment of a Person's Persona.

99. You Should Always Live Your Life Before You Die.

100. If You Can't get into you Own head, How can you get into Someone Else's.

3

INSPIRATIONS

What ever will be will be when it is time for it to be.

1. Is being in a Gang where Cowards go to hide?

2. Every man should take time to be a Dad if that is the Case.

3. In the Game of Life are the only Winners the Survivors?

4. A good man makes a good woman.

5. Life is like a math problem. Youi have to work it till you get it right.

6. You can never own a child of God.

7. Do you ever think that I think that you think what I am thinking?

8. The bigger a person becomes, the less you will say no to them.

9. How do you know what to look for when you don't know what you lost?

10. Can you see the pain that I feel?

11. Our destiny is described by the decisions that we make.

12. Sometimes we have to touch the bottom to reach the top.

13. Each year that you have a birthday is a privilege that can only be lived once.

14. The thing about life is you have to try to figure out how to get the best out of it.

15. If you can't deal with your own problems, how can you deal with other people's problems?

16. The best way to learn is to see it, hear it, understand and believe it. Then keep on practicing it.

17. You can be Rich on earth, and not make it to Heaven because you don't want to give up your Earthly goods and follow the Word of God.

18. When you come out of the darkness run to the light and don't look back, because the day you look back that us the day you go back.

19. To change your perspectives, first you have to Change.

20. To see a new discovery you first have to see it with new eyes.

21. In the End, the only thing that matters is what Really Matters.

22. If your gut says one thing and your heart says another, Always follow your heart.

23. Today, if Jesus came down from Heaven and told me, if I was a Rich man, to leave my Reaches on earth and go with him, I would be gone.

24. What makes a clown great is when you don't see the Hurt behind the Masquerade.

25. When you don't see it like That, you won't remember it like That.

26. Sharing a vision from the past is a really good thing but when it is Really good, it is Beautiful.

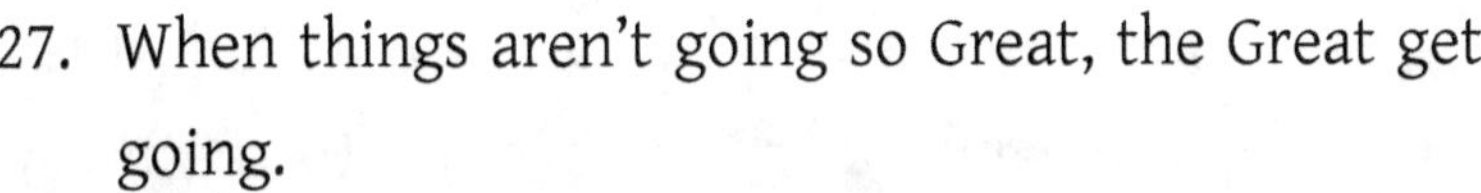

27. When things aren't going so Great, the Great get going.

28. Age makes us Wiser, but to get Wise, we have to Age.

29. Coffee will still be Black Until you put some Cream and Sugar in it.

30. Until We Change Things around, Things will Remain the Same.

31. Your Faith, should Never be Broken.

32. The Deadliest form of Denial is when you Delay into Doing Something.

33. When you Miss Something, you will Always think about your last time.

34. If you believe in Faith, you don't Need Proof. If you don't believe, no Proof is Possible.

35. The Sabbath of the Lord was made for man to Rest. People today go to church on Sunday, the day that the Ancient Pagan's worshipped the Sun God. Jesus died on Friday and rested on Saturday.

36. Don't be so desperate to get what you want, that you sell your soul.

37. If we understand with Age, we should learn in our youth.

38. If a man is running away from you, how is he a threat, Officer?

39. Life is like a puzzle, you have to find the right pieces and put them together to see the whole picture.

40. Only the misguided will be stuck in the mud of Satan's entrapments.

41. To find out where you came/come from, you first have to find your gynecology.

42. Your love makes up for my imperfections.

43. No matter how innocent we are, Evil will always come into our lives.

44. Deep down inside we all are capable of unspeakable acts.

45. Some people don't believe until something happens.

46. They say that only God knows why people do what they do, but the Devil also knows.

47. When you are looking on the inside, from the inside, you still can miss the Truth.

48. When you are looking from the outside in, you only see half of what's going on.

49. Believe me I know the concept of having your cake and eating it too. But if it's Your cake you should be able to eat it.

50. Sometimes do you feel too young to be old and too old to be young?

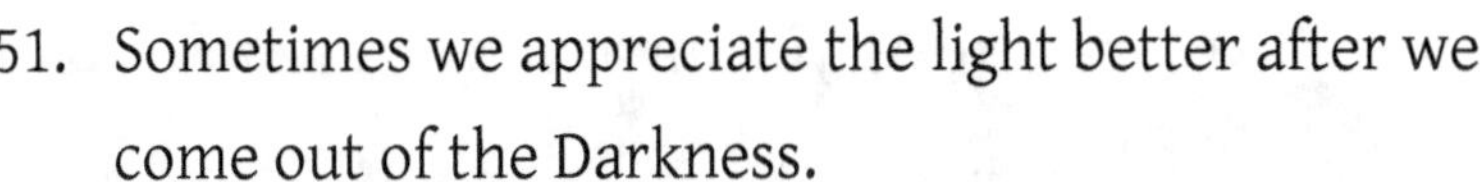

51. Sometimes we appreciate the light better after we come out of the Darkness.

52. At some time in our lives the bad things can overtake the good things.

53. Life is like big box of candy, you get an assortment of flavors but you won't know what you're getting until you take a bite out of a piece.

54. When desire overtakes reason, the human mind can go astray.

55. If someone kneels for You, you must stand for Them.

56. You can be wrong the last time but right this time.

57. Remember when the Lord sends you through troubled waters; it might be because your enemy's can't swim.

58. If you don't want to be on your butt, then stand up on your feet.

59. Most of the time we look like the way we live.

60. We should never abandon any search for the Truth.

61. When reasoning fails, man will use force to prevail.

62. It is Always better to be on This side of the law, than That side.

63. No one can shackle the Hope that abides in our hearts.

64. Sometimes a Bad start is a means to a Good End.

65. To be Great, you first have to go far past the Standard.

66. A Soul without Faith is a Soul Lost.

67. Even in the darkest of places, Hope can be found.

68. I will follow my Conscience not man's law.

69. If you have your ticket, you should be able to ride.

70. Some of us want to ride that Heavenly Train in the morning.

71. Today never Stops. It is Always Creeping toward Tomorrow.

72. Upon our own skins we are confined for Life to Solitary Confinement.

73. If you have Never done research on a subject, then shut up and Listen.

74. No matter what, you are Never too old to Learn.

75. Sometimes when people can't find fault, they create it.

76. If you can see with new eyes, you can see a new Horizon.

77. If you think the Possible, you can overcome the Impossible.

78. Some of us know things and some of us don't, but in between there is perception.

79. If our relationship Ever gets Strained, I will Never talk to you Until You talk to me.

80. To be good at Anything, you must pay the Price.

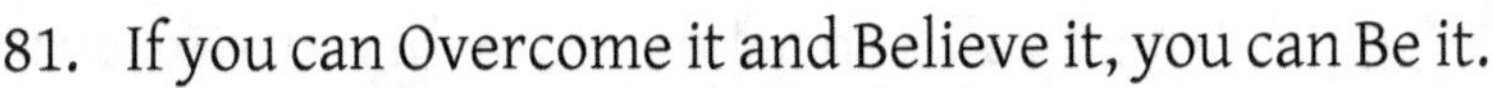

81. If you can Overcome it and Believe it, you can Be it.

82. Where there is Life, there is also Death.

83. If you accept Life, then you must accept the Death that soon follows.

84. Our life is not just about what we do for people. It is about the Love we put into what we do for people.

85. Sometimes I Need you to Really Hear what I Need to Say.

86. When we talk about the Haves and the Have Nots, the Rich think that Some can Have and Some Cannot. They think it's not enough to go around.

87. Sometimes when you want a little sumin, sumin. You have to give a little sumin, sumin. Or, in lay-men's terms. If you want something, you have to give something. It's called Quid, Pro, Quo. That's Latin for, You do something for me, and I will do something for you.

88. When you want to go Anywhere in this world, All you have to do is put one step in front of the other and keep on stepping until you get there.

89. Our Lord Thy God helps those, who helps those, who help those.

90. The Lord Thy God is a server of those who serve.

91. Don't ever be afraid of love. Life is too short. Think it over. Like Bobby Womack said, that's the way I feel about it.

92. A man called by the Lord is here to Teach, Lead, and Love.

93. Some folks can't stand for you to be right about them being wrong.

94. The Lord's justice will Never Sleep. Vengeance will be his.

95. If it wasn't right yesterday, it won't be right today.

96. I am a little piece of leather, but I am well put together. But I will fight on the side of the Lord All the days of my Life.

97. When Moses' came down from Mt Sinai, some of his people were going against the God of Israel, Worshipping a Golden Pagan Image of a Calf. So Moses' told his people whoever is on the side of the Lord come unto me. Then the one's that stayed fast was the wicked, and they were destroyed by the fiery vengeance of Our Lord. Beware America. You are now the wicked. Beware of the Lake of Fire.

98. Don't just listen and believe in others. You have to find out for yourself.

99. Sometime when your Husband is the Boss, He must have the Sauce.

100. I am So Competitive, I will fight until the Dawn's early light, to get it Right.

INSPIRATIONS

Should I Oppose you that Oppose me?

1.   You do what you need to do, and I am going to do what I need to do.

2.   I will see you in Heaven or Hell. I just want you to get there before I do.

3.   I find it funny but true, that the light makes us dark, and the dark makes us light.

4.   I am a good neighbor and I am not affiliated with State Farm.

5.   When you and the Devil fight against the Righteous, the Lord Thy God Will Always Prevail.

6.   If you live with me, you should know me and learn to understand me.

7.   Big or small, a lie will never equal the Truth.

8.   A good education gives us the possibility to change things.

9.   You can dance with the Devil or choose to sleep alone.

10. You have to have a finger up on a thumbs down person.

11. If a book is not interesting, you won't turn the page.

12. If you don't find the Solution to the Problem, you will continue to have that Problem.

13. If Hate can put you in prison, Love can bust you out.

14. A detective's job is to go into the Darkness and bring the Truth to the Light.

15. For your conscience mind, it is better for you to know rather than for you not to know.

16. When you violate your parole, you and only you shall pay.

17. All humans should live by one Divine Commandment and not by Man's Earthly Doctrine. But by Our Creator a Divine Spirit being the Lord Thy God.

18. The sun is Always shining somewhere on this Great Earth. So it is Always shining somewhere.

19. We should always study our lessons with ambition because that always shows our character.

20. You have to know what I am Talking about, to Know what I am Talking about.

21. When you pick up a book, and start to read. What makes you turn the page?

22. Sometimes you don't know until you know.

23. Don't try to save your children from life. Let them live it.

24. When you always do the right thing, you may be called a righteous person.

25. No matter what the others do, Always choose what's best for you.

26. The Lord Thy God did not create people to be Evil, (Satan) the Devil did.

27. If you are in law enforcement you can't always think about the ones you can't catch, you think about the ones you're going to save.

28. Sometimes you don't want to come down from your cloud.

29. I am sorry for many things, but I will never be sorry for loving you.

30. Life should be about looking in not out, looking up and not down, looking forward and not backwards.

31. When we walk, we make a small carbon footprint.

32. A Great man achieves Great things in a Great way.

33. Followers always follow because they aren't ambitious to lead.

34. Even in certain situations when things don't go right, some people say they are just going by the book to do their job. I say in that case or situation you need a new book.

35. It's not good to live in the past, but sometimes we have to visit.

36. Sometimes your hatred of me, makes me hate you.

37. Everybody has their own stories to tell. Would you listen to one of mine?

38. Once upon a time there was but now is just another time.

39. If you are in good hands, do you trust and have faith in them?

40. You are you and I am me, and that is the way God wants us to be.

41. Sometimes new eyes can see a lot more than old ones.

42. When I was a childish lad, I thought like a kid. Now that I am a grown man, I think like a wise old owl.

43. Anyone with a ghost in their mind has a dangerous mind.

44. You should never ever stop, until you get there.

45. For the sake of my family, my journey continues.

46. I'm like a hungry, hungry hippo. I keep grabbing at a dream.

47. If you say that you loved me yesterday, then you say that you hate me today, will you love me again tomorrow?

48. Like a diamond needs pressure to exist, we as humans need to exist by our struggle with pressure in our lives.

49. The Devil lives in Darkness and our Lord lives in Light.

50. If seeing is believing, then tell me why can't some people see the Truth?

51. This is a game that we choose to play, so we play it.

52. When you are still under the Yoke of your Oppressor, you are not truly Free.

53. One and one, is always going to be two. Two and two, is always going to be four. So don't ever run from the Truth.

54. I did the wrong Thing, for the wrong Reason, at the wrong Time.

55. Sometimes we say that coincidences happen, but if it is really true, it is not a coincidence.

56. It might seem impossible now, but when you do it, you know.

57. In the middle of knowing and unknowing is perception.

58. If you believe it, you can become it. It is your vision in life.

59. When I was a child, I was taught to go against the American Indian as the culprit, when he fought against the Western Cowboy. But when I grew up, I found that it was the opposite. The Cowboy was the culprit all the time.

60. We know how to play your game. Now do you know how to play ours?

61. It's hard to stay up while trying to keep someone else up.

62. You can run from man, woman, the Truth, the Devil and even the Lord Thy God, but you can't run from yourself.

63. We should never let enmity and strife confound our lives.

64. If you believe in the Lord, he will Smite Thy Enemies with his mighty Sword.

65. Our Lord is a loving God, and he loves a lot of things but he does not love Sin or Sinners.

66. Sometimes it's just a thread that holds a family together.

67. We all will either be rewarded or punished for the choices that we make in our lives.

68. Sometimes we celebrate prematurely. But I say you can't celebrate before the Fat Lady Sings. Even if she stands up to clear her throat, you have to wait till she Sings.

69. No matter what, man cannot forgive man. Only our Lord and Savior can do that.

70. You cannot atone for the sins of your Ancestors.

71. You cannot commit to sins through the week and ask for forgiveness on Saturday or Sunday and expect the Lord to Forgive you. That is what Satan wants you to think.

72. If you walk the walk, and win you can talk the talk. If you lose, you shouldn't say anything.

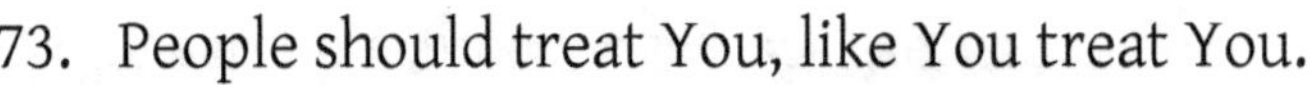

73. People should treat You, like You treat You.

74. Sometimes we need to be led to the Light.

75. With Amazing Grace, if you were lost and now found, why would you ever be lost again?

76. Today I understand, whereas yesterday, I did not.

77. Every one of us on this planet is responsible for his actions.

78. If you are guilty of a crime, shall you always be forgiven?

79. Be with me Lord, when I walk through that shadow of Death.

80. Dawn has come for over a thousand centuries and tomorrow, without fail, it Shall come again.

81. I like to help the people that helped me and I like to help people that need help.

82. I am a caregiver not a caretaker. I don't take care, I give care.

83. Sometimes people that have been hurt the most, have the greater possibility to heal.

84. Why should we be sorry for other people's woes?

85. Loyalty is a scarce commodity in the business of gang members.

86. If we keep looking back, we will miss our whole life.

87. After all is said and done, at the end of the day we decide who we are.

88. Our behaviors really show our true image.

89. I can say that I am a man of God. God can say he is a God of man.

90. When you lay in the bosom of the Lord Thy God, you are in the perfect hands.

91. If you want to find out if someone has skeletons in their closet, you should look in their closet.

92. If you have skeletons in your closet, you should clean your closet.

93. Some think that Love never dies a natural death.

94. Every origin on earth has a story to tell.

95. Sometimes people are like a shadow. You can tell their shapes but not their color, character, or identity.

96. What I like about athletics is, we go from being down to being up. Then go from being up to being down again. Then going from being down to going back up.

97. If you ever bite the hand that feeds you, then you shouldn't be fed.

98. Can we all learn to trust someone that is not trustworthy?

99. No matter what you say, none of us are here to stay.

INSPIRATIONS

If you love me, let me know. If you love me, it will show.

1. Who knows where inspiration comes from? Does it come from the life we choose to live or the life others choose to live?
2. Sometimes when people ask me what's up, I tell them the Sun and my blood pressure.
3. Hear no evil. See no evil. Believe no gossip.
4. Sometimes we rely on assumption and that could be called, racial profiling or behavioral profiling.
5. Sometimes the messenger might also receive a message.
6. The key to making a relationship work is to making sure you have one in the first place.
7. We all are relieved when we see the end of the road after a good hard travel.
8. I want you to know how I feel and what I think, so I write.
9. Don't ever refuse help from someone, because of shame. Think first, you can always use that to help others.
10. When you go to sea, you see what sailors see.
11. I have heard all my life that the customer is always right. Not in my book. If you are wrong, how can you be right?
12. When you sign a pact with the Devil, he wants you to pay your dues every time.
13. Your life means something in my life.

14. In the Navy, you never know where you're going until you get there.

15. Any time we fight Evil with Evil, Evil will Always Win.

16. Sometimes when you want to trap the Devil you have to play with his Demons.

17. Some say you have to stand on one side of the fence or the other side. I then say, if you don't know what side of the fence to stand on, then just tear down the fence.

18. No society stays the same. Either you grow with it or you die with it.

19. Marriage is always like give and take. Some days you have to give a lot and take a little and sometimes you give a little and take a lot.

20. You can't follow the Devil, and expect to go to Heaven.

21. I don't mind being wealthy, I just don't want to be rich.

22. Sometimes I feel bad for what I did, but I don' regret what I did.

23. Sometimes you have to look back at where you were, to find out where you're going.

24. Some people like to be alone when they have a lot of thinking to do.

25. If you have to have a reason for everything that happens, you might just go crazy.

26. Sometimes you have to believe that there is no Earthly answer.

27. Some people use the new to get rid of the old.

28. You will always have to stop the delusions to conquer your fear of the Truth.

29. Sometimes you have to do this to get that. And sometimes you have to do that to get this.

30. It's not really funny but it is crazy, that, the God of Light, who is Satan the Devil, lives in the Darkness of Sin.

31. When they start fighting Oh Lord, I hope I am with You.

32. How can you get kicked out of Heaven for not paying your rent?

33. One time a poor man that had just become rich told me that old friends and relatives kept asking him for money. So he got tired of that and told them that, if I gave every one that asked me for a dollar, I would not even have one dollar.

34. If you never get on the playing field, how can you play?

35. If you never get on the playing field, you cannot play.

36. Most people should shut the f—k up, and sit the f—k down.

37. Young or old, the Truth should never harm anyone.

38. Sometimes avoidance is what some people do best.

39. We always say divide and conquer. I say, divide to conquer.

40. Sometimes we can say, here we go and here we come at the same time, when we are trying to succeed.

41. When you live in a nest, to get out you have to fall out or fly out.

42. Believe it or not, your happiness is my happiness.

43. Before you can knock the ball out of the ballpark, you first have to get in the game.

44. You are never lost if you follow the Spirit of Our Lord.

45. Walk in the footsteps of Jesus and you shall be saved.

46. When you are taught to Teach, and you Teach, I will call you Teacher.

47. A perverted mind only creates perversion.

48. I want to see what I seen yesterday to make sure I seen what I saw.

49. Sometimes we need to just sit down, listen, and learn.

50. Don't settle for crumbs when you can have the whole loaf.

51. Our Lord God loves the just, as well as the unjust. He just loves the just a little bit more for their obedience.

52. We all have to make choices in our lifetime so sometimes we have to decide by ourselves, what choice to make.

53. You can conform to man's doctrine while on this Earth but remember your Spirit has to answer to God's.

54. Humans are the only Homo sapiens that let their emotions cloud their way of thinking.

55. I like people to know what I am talking about when I am talking about what I am talking about.

56. Because of what I am talking about, I want you to know when I am talking about what I am talking about; I just want to know if you really know what I am saying.

57. I've always heard that Father knows best. But I will say that Mother knows the Rest.

58. Every time we wake up in the morning and thank the Lord God, for another day, he is happy. But the Devil is mad at us because we still have a chance to skip Hell and make it to Heaven.

59. People will sometimes come up to me and ask me how do I come up with the word that I come up with? I tell them that I just write down what I think.

60. I don't have to make anything up in my life because the Truth is Never made up.

61. Only a lie is made up because it is not made of the Truth.

62. I like to inspire your desire to get a little bit higher.

63. When bad cops shoot unarmed and innocent people, I still hear some folks say what the victim should have done. I say as a military veteran, they were trained to do no harm to innocent civilians. It should be about what they shouldn't have done.

64. If you as a parent teach your children not to do something that you are doing in front of their face, they will do the same thing behind your back.

65. Sometimes we have to appreciate the kind things that people do for us, so they will appreciate our appreciation. And sometimes, we have to let them know that we appreciate that appreciation.

66. Our human brain is a station of memories, cognizance, and coordination. It also controls the body's actions, reactions and functions that also, allow us to think and feel.

67. What your brain thinks and eyes see, can be very different.

68. Evil wants us to know it is Spectacular. It lives with us, breathes with us, and dies with us. It lives at our dinner table.

69. Technology that does not work should be labeled as abstract. Theoretically separately from something else.

70. If you exist in a thought or an idea, and don't have a physical or concrete existence, you might just be labeled as an abstract person.

71. If you want us to go back to Africa, where we have never been, then why don't you can go back to Europe?

72. If I am sick that it is eminent that I will soon die, I won't want you to see me die, but to see me dead is a different story.

73. People are talking about Blacks kneeling or standing for the national anthem. But our government recognizes, but, doesn't stop the Neo Nazi, White Supremacist, White Skin Heads, and the KKK from terrorizing Black Americans, while marching down main St. America, How can you talk? It is 2017, and Whites still mess with Blacks. Get over it folks. Whites have been prejudiced against Blacks for over 500 years.

74. Most of the time, the force behind every successful man, is a strong woman.

75. Some people know what's happening, because they go thru what is happening.

76. If you plan to fight against the establishment, you first have to establish a plan to fight.

77. I will Never apologize for telling the Truth.

78. I don't believe in apologizes, because I say what I mean and I mean what I say and I mean what I do.

79. My God has said that there is a Devil. So if we believe in God, we must believe that there is a Devil.

80. If every minute, you will disappear, a little for hating someone, would you totally disappear?

81. Racism has always been here. It has just adjusted for the times.

82. You can enslave my body for a minute, but you will Never enslave my Mind.

83. With my Word I am a man, therefore, I am a man of my Word.

84. Man has a very hard time remembering things from the past, and some men have a hard time keeping memories from their pants.

85. If you do it like this, it could come out like that. If you do it like that, it could come out like this.

86. If you do it like this, it's going to come out like this. If you do it like that, it will come out like that.

87. We live, we grow, we learn, we fall and then we Rise.

88. When the Devil brings depression, despair, and sorrow to your door and you don't give him a seat he will bring his own stool. Then you have to kick that stool from under him.

89. I don't care who you are. If I don't receive any Respect from you, you won't get any Respect from me.

90. We must remember that men died for us to Stand for our National Anthem and they also died for us to Sit.

91. If a man cheats on his spouse, you can still call him a man. If a woman cheats on her spouse, you can't call her a lady.

92. Good people are Always worth listening to.

93. No one is way beyond Growing.

94. How can you try to Save the world and break bread with someone who wants to Destroy it?

95. You can cry all you want, but when your tears are gone, life will still go on.

96. Fighting is not just about winning, it is about discipline.

97. If you believe it then do it and become it.

98. If you think one way, and you don't really know the truth, should you teach your child that way?

99. It will always be two sides of a fence. You have to know the history of both sides to determine what side you want to be on.

100. If God is the Glory, then the Glory is God.

3
INSPIRATIONS

One for the money, two for the show, when I am ready I will go.

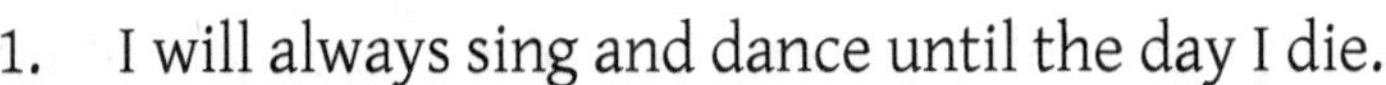

1. I will always sing and dance until the day I die.

2. Sometimes you just have to bet on yourself.

3. If your friends heighten your pain when they are in your presence, they are not really your friends.

4. Bullshit never stops. It will even come to you in your sleep.

5. If you ever have a Setback, you have to make a Comeback.

6. We are going to do this, With our people. We are going to do this, To our people. And at last, we are going to do this, For our people. Only if we are in Unity.

7. You can get away with it for years. But when you are finally caught, you did not get away with it at all.

8. Do you know I mean? I mean what I say and I mean what I do.

9. When you get knocked down and fail to get up, you fail yourself and you fail your children.

10. O. If ever you find someone good in this world, whether it is a friend or lover, You better hold on for the long haul.

11. Only the rains will know when the flowers will grow.

12. If we humans don't show our emotions long enough, we just might lose them.

13. First you have to trust. Then you will find out if you should have trusted.

14. Inspiration to me means that you believe in something beautiful can and will happen to you.

15. When you lie to someone you lose a little of your reality.

16. Remember the Sabbath, is the fourth commandment. God created this world in six days and rested on the seventh. They say that Jesus obeyed this. He died on Friday, rested on Saturday (the Sabbath) and rose on Sunday to do the Lord's bidding. If that is true, why do people worship on Sunday?

17. If it doesn't matter what day we worship on, why does the Lord tell us to Remember?

18. I don't want to save your life. I want to save your soul.

19. There is a conscience that dwells in each and every one of us.

20. Going beyond, is not assuming what is, but it is knowing, what is.

21. Do not ever erase your identifier. It is yours from birth.

22. Sometimes we love what we do, so we do what we love.

23. Sometimes I sit and wonder where do dreams go to die.

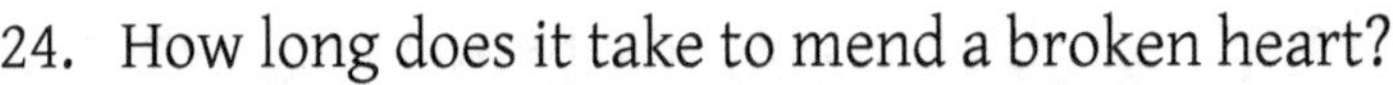

24. How long does it take to mend a broken heart?

25. You might forget how you want to say something, but you must never forget what you want to say.

26. Tell me where do broken hearts go to live?

27. If I am a loner, am I anti-social or self-reliant?

28. First we learn the lesson. Then we take the test.

29. My feet may leave my home, but my heart will always be there.

30. It's a shame when your government writes off its citizens, instead of sacrificing its national interests.

31. I had a saying in High School when I was playing football. If I can touch it, I can catch it.

32. Death never waits for you to say thank you, I love you or goodbye.

33. If you lose it all you might then understand it all.

34. We all have to come to a cross in the road of life. It is called the cross roads. When You get there, which way are You going to go, left or right?

35. Sometimes you can make a way with no way.

36. We can never compare man's knowledge of life to the wisdom of God.

37. If You deny me My freedom, then You do not deserve it.

38. We all need to be seen and to be who we really are.

39. When it comes to your children you can't always say nay, but you shouldn't always say yay.

40. Your friend today could be your enemy tomorrow.

41. Your parents see you into this world, and we might have to see them out of this world.

42. If God ever takes you into troubled waters, it is not to drown you, but to cleanse you.

43. We have to know that, when we get up on age, time moves one way, and memory moves another.

44. As a team, we play together to win or we play together and lose.

45. I can love your body but hate your characteristics.

46. Love comes in all kinds of colors and flavors.

47. If you have a body for sin, you should have a head for business.

48. Blessed be the true followers of Jesus, for in the end, we will be the chosen ones.

49. Sometimes we don't have to change what we do, but change how much we do what we do.

50. I have always thought that people, like circumstances; change, so we should learn to adapt to the new change of circumstances.

51. If we don't find a way to love, we will die in our hatred.

52. How can you hate a people when you don't even know them?

53. Speaking of love at first sight, you have to like a person before you love them.

54. Your Mind can be in it. Your Heart can be in it. But if your body is not in it you will have trouble winning anything.

55. When you keep secrets about anything, what does that say about you?

56. If you ever chase your dreams, don't ever stop.

57. Don't imagine what I should be about. Just imagine what I am about.

58. To me, Love is from your heart and not your mind.

59. Being blessed means that you can't have a bowl of cherries every time, but you stay around to eat a few.

60. As long as people and things stay the same, they will never change.

61. Sometimes we don't live in the past; it is still right here.

62. God may hate the sin but he still loves the sinner.

63. We can become an unstoppable force if we could just unite as Black and White.

64. Sometimes some type of success is a type of failure.

65. Thru your lifetime, you can live, laugh, and love but most of all you have to learn.

66. Our skin color may be different, but our souls are created the same.

67. No healing can begin without someone being held accountable.

68. Sometimes it isn't a matter of conflict between good and evil, it is really between the truth and the untruth.

69. We all have the responsible rights for life, liberty and the pursuit happily intoxicated.

70. The Devil may take tomorrow, but today I have Jesus.

71. Any time the risk is worth the benefit; go with the risk.

72. Some folks believe in Christianity and some Believe in Spirituality.

73. When it is time to get busy, that is when you get busy.

74. If you Ever ask for one more of Anything, you are in Need.

75. I think that the Only Master you should have in this world is the Lord Thy God.

76. Don't ever let one person bring you down because of their disparity. Keep on believing in yourself.

77. Sometimes we have to let go to possess what is truly ours.

78. No matter what path you take in this life, you must always be True to yourself.

79. Sometimes I sit and ask myself, what am I doing here? Only God knows the True answer.

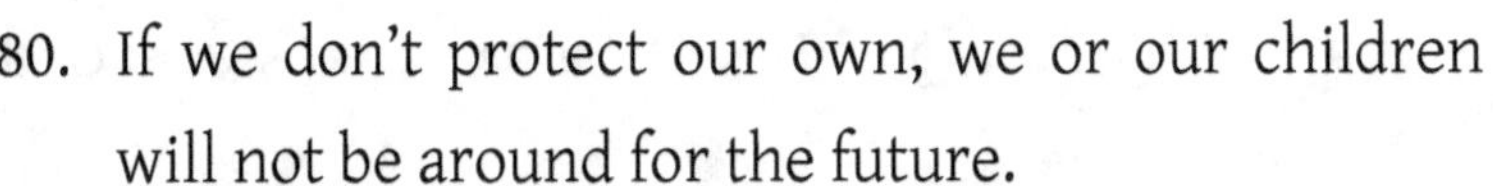

80. If we don't protect our own, we or our children will not be around for the future.

81. No matter what, you cannot own a child of God.

82. Sometimes I need you to let me do what I need to do to win.

83. Don't let who I was yesteryear, compare to who I am today.

84. To increase your face value you must grin, smile and laugh.

85. Sometimes we have to pay attention to what is, forget about what was and have faith in what's to come.

86. Evil and Darkness is always a whisper away.

87. If you can't change it then let it go to someone else.

88. If you have experienced the Goodness and the Greatness and the Mercy of God without seeing him, your faith is on point.

89. When we make bad choices in life it doesn't mean we are bad.

90. If you still have a friend from Elementary School, it is because there is no Expiration date on True Friendship.

91. True lovers stick together, love together, laugh together, cry together, learn together and grow together.

92. Whatever the Devil (Satan) can steal, God can restore.

93. If you want to survive the storms of life, you must build your life around a strong foundation.

94. Sometimes we all have to go into the fire and come out like a Phoenix.

95. If you go into the fire and come out alive; you will come out on fire.

96. Because I drink and talk the Truth, does that diminish what I say?

97. It's a shame that when you are in a rut, no one helps you out.

98. It's nothing we could do without love, because love can change the world.

99. What some people need to know that in our lifetime, the Story of Us can include Them.

100. When you change your clothing, you change your ideology.

INSPIRATIONS

Let no one be left behind that deserves to go forward.

1. If we are not our brother's keepers, then who should we keep?

2. When you open your heart to me, I will open my heart to you.

3. When you open your heart to someone, you give them an opportunity to open up to you.

4. A voice of Unity should Always be Heard.

5. I am like Yogi Bear. I am not the average kind of Bear.

6. If you ask for forgiveness for anything, should you not be forgiven?

7. We all should grow out of a Spirit of Cooperation.

8. Someone out there always knows the truth.

9. Sometimes people talk and they don't know and some people know and they don't talk.

10. If you say it and believe it and then you know it, you can do it.

11. If you don't put in the work, you don't get the reward.

12. To be the Champ, you have to beat the Champ.

13. There are things unknown and there are things known.

14. You know what you believe and you believe what you know.

15. Knowing is just half of the Battle.

16. In between time and in the meantime, you can do your thang and I will do mine.

17. If it's your thang, you should do what you like to do.

18. I don't believe in love at first sight. You have to know someone before you like them. Therefore, you have to like someone before you love them.

19. We have a certain feeling when we meet someone in life. You feel in like, you feel in love, and now you are husband and wife.

20. Sometimes you don't lose a war, you just don't win it.

21. When it comes to he said she said, don't blame me until you know the Truth.

22. To me, women that are married and like to keep their maiden name with their new married name; want to hold on to the past.

23. The Devil (Satan) always has a way of doing bad things.

24. American life might have stopped Kunta Kinte, but it won't stop me.

25. If I can control your thinking, I can control your emotions.

26. If cops can't serve and protect everyone, then don't serve.

27. Sometimes we have to help people that can't help themselves.

28. Some people have everything to lose and some have everything to prove.

29. There is no difference in large or small problems, when it comes to Truth and Justice.

30. Just be thankful that you can be thankful.

31. When you find your feet are firmly planted you will also find that you are in the right place.

32. Sometimes we have to carry someone else's message.

33. Our technology today captures and records your personal information in seconds; don't do anything that is embarrassing or regretful.

34. Sometimes it is bad news for someone else but good news for you.

35. You have to be on the right path to be up with Jesus.

36. If I say something that you don't believe in, you have the right to a rebuttal. But I have the right to rebut your rebuttal.

37. This is what you people who think the world owes you anything or something. A Big O will show up. A Goose Egg is what you will get in the end.

38. When we look at any photo of something or someone, we can't tell if it or they are hiding secrets.

39. Don't just read my works, and follow my works, believe in my works because they are Inspirational and True.

40. Pain and suffering is what you will get in the end when the truth comes out to be Karma.

41. If you love your freedom; don't ever get locked up, or go to jail or prison.

42. Sometimes when we are young, we dream; and as we grow older we may find that we can't fulfill that dream, so we just dream another dream.

43. A smile can come across your face because of your tone.

44. The key to good communication is not being a good talker; it is being a good listener.

45. Sometimes you can respectfully agree to disagree.

46. When everything is quiet, there is a peace within.

47. Sometimes a perfect ending is really just a perfect beginning.

48. Yesterday we thought about tomorrow and now it is here today.

49. If you are evil you will honor the God of evil which is Lucifer.

50. Lucifer was kicked out of Heaven because he didn't pay his rent.

51. So if you don't pay your rent to our Lord thy God, you will not live in the Kingdom of Heaven.

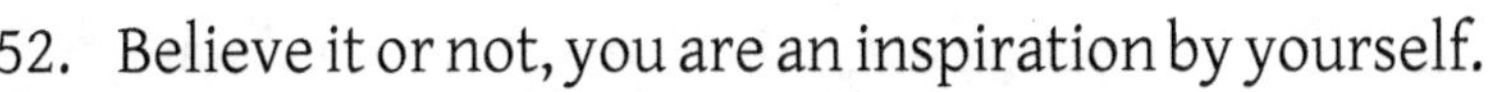
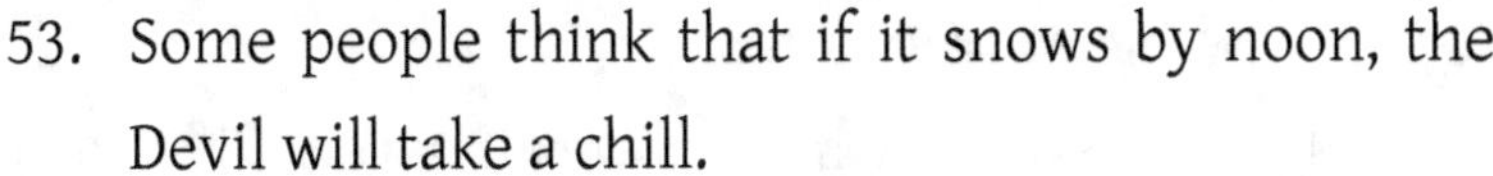

52. Believe it or not, you are an inspiration by yourself.

53. Some people think that if it snows by noon, the Devil will take a chill.

54. Where there is a good there is a bad. Where there is a Black there is a White. Where there is an up there is a down. Where there is an in there is an out.

55. One thing about trouble, it Never takes a day off.

56. You can't have a shadow without a light.

57. You need this, or you want that. A need will exceed a want every time.

58. Sometimes you need to make time to treat yourself.

59. The more you read, the more you will understand someone else's emotions.

60. If you read my books, you will feel and hear my stories.

61. If you can get it there, I will catch it there.

62. I'd love you to like me and I'd like you to love me.

63. If you like me you will know me and if you know me you will like me.

64. If you need a friend to the very end; I'll be by your side.

65. Our parents take care of us at our early age. We then, take care of them at their older age.

66. If it is in your head, it could be in your heart.

67. When it is time to shine, just turn on your light.

68. You are you and I am me so when we are together we are you and me.

69. This is a crazy life but we all have to live with it.

70. Can you ever tell someone what something is about without telling the whole story?

71. We all have to change things for the better.

72. Is luxury the height of your own sky?

73. I might talk a lot of stuff, but I don't take a lot of stuff.

74. In the meantime and in between time, you will do your thang and I will do mine.

75. Love sometimes will not bring us together.

76. The greatest threat to a family may come from within the family.

77. With fishing you have to wait for the fish to bite. In life you have to go after what you want.

78. Some people see and judge you by where you come from.

79. For a man it's his and for a woman it's hers. So why do we call it a hysterectomy when a woman gets fixed and not her-ectomy?

80. When it comes to masquerading, sometimes we have to unmask before midnight.

81. When we tell the Truth, the Devil runs away in shame.

82. Bad friends are like diabetes. Sometimes you will have poor circulation to the point you have to cut off a body part.

83. Sometimes when we are innocent, we are still found guilty.

84. You can't keep telling a woman no and expect to keep her.

85. When it comes down to having fun, everyone should have them some.

86. Time has it's time. You got yours, and I got mine.

87. Sometimes someone's misery is someone else's mission in life.

88. I love the sunrise because it is the beginning of a new day. I love the sunset because it is the ending of a new day

89. No matter what race you belong to; big, small, short or tall, we All will be judged on Judgement day by Jesus Christ our Lord and Savior.

90. A nightmare can be in Black and White but a True Dream should be in Living Color.

91. No matter what your race is we are All Human Beings.

92. Sometimes we just have to break thru all those barriers of the past like they never existed.

93. You will find me at my finest if our paths ever crossed.

94. People that don't listen will sometimes lose out.

95. Life will bring us many things like, sorrow, pain, misery, hatefulness, gluttony, greed, prejudice, happiness, love and joy.

96. Once I was a child, dreaming about space and now I am a man wondering about space. One day, I would like to see space.

97. If your Oppressor gets rich off of your suffering, then you have to Stop the Oppression.

98. You can't let time disappear when there is no time to waste.

99. In the past we were kids. In the present we are youngsters. In the future we will grow to be grown adults.

100. Judge me not until All my work is done.

10
INSPIRATIONS

When we reach out and teach we can inspire. Our work and our music is never forgotten.

1. Home is where you feel safe and sound.

2. Sometimes we have to make Calm out of Kayos.

3. No one is sinless and perfect except Jesus Christ our Lord and Savior.

4. Why does this mean that and that means this?

5. You can be like a bee with honey on your mouth and a Sting in your Tail.

6. Intelligence and awareness doesn't always allow us to control our urges to commit acts of passion.

7. Who we are is constantly evolving. I am not the man that I was ten years ago and neither are you.

8. Most secrets are deep and dark.

9. Once the dam breaks the flood is always right behind.

10. Everybody needs someone to lean on.

11. We must Always Remember that in some Communications, Connections Fail and Relationships Die.

12. Sometimes we become parents to our parents.

13. Remember when working outside the box, the box is there for a reason.

14. We live with a lot of problems that are real and present. So never bring imagined ones to your table.

15. The truth about discoveries is they never end.

16. We all have Flashbacks of the Good and the Bad times of the past.

17. Hoping that All of my FB Fam, Friends and Relatives have a Safe and Merry Christmas. And Remember, when U Really, Really Believe, U will Never take CHRIST out of CHRISTMAS!!!

18. Don't ever dwell on the bad things in your life. The good could soon take over and make you forget about the bad.

19. As we grow in life our little dreams grow with our age. I am at the age now of having very big dreams.

20. People must remember, when handling business, your business is nobodies but yours. My business is my business.

21. If you make the wine, I will drink it.

22. All of us together can make the Impossible, Possible.

23. Life may not be forever but Love is.

24. When it comes to losing weight, it is sometimes not about losing the weight; it is about what you gain when you lose it.

25. Sometimes we play a game when things aren't fine. If I have your back, you better have mine.

26. Who cares what you think about me when you didn't care about me in the first place?

27. Sometimes forgiveness starts with forgiving ourselves.

28. We often say that it pays to have high friends in low places.

29. If I can't help you when I want, I will, help you when I can.

30. Sometimes you do it this way and that way and it doesn't work; so then you have to do it the other way or another way.

31. Keep studying until you find the Exact Truth.

32. If you are looking for something, you might just find it if you don't stop looking.

33. When we are young, we should learn by example or experience; so by the time we are older, we Understand.

34. If you don't understand, then you can't. If you don't believe, then you won't. If you do understand, then you can. And if you really, Truly believe, then you will.

35. Even Satan (The Devil) Believes in Our Lord Thy God.

36. If I can you can and if you can we all can.

37. Sometimes it's not all about the Destination; it's Sometimes about the Journey.

38. When you talk to a talker, the talker should listen to you and you should listen to the talker.

39. Don't just imagine what I can do; See what I can do.

40. When we fight against Evil and Evil wins, it is a Temporary Fix. In the end Good will outdo Evil Every time.

41. Our opinions only last a skinnet and that is quicker than a minute. Facts last a whole lifetime.

42. It is said that instead of Strict Justice; we All should bear the Fruits of Mercy.

43. Sometimes with twins; the Fate of One will be placed into the hands of the Other.

44. Yesterday we wondered. Today we Experienced. Tomorrow we Learn so in the Future we teach.

45. All I want to do in life is have the Lord help me help others see the Light In the name of Jesus.

46. No matter how old we are on this Earth, we All need Strength, Wisdom, and Guidance to see us through our Life.

47. To be gentle you have to be Strong. To be strong you have to be Gentle.

48. Sometimes we have to Serve the Servers to receive Honor and Respect from our Servers.

49. If you Love me tell me, so I will Cherish your Love.

50. Life is Really short; so do and enjoy life at the fullest because you only get that chance that the Creator gives you.

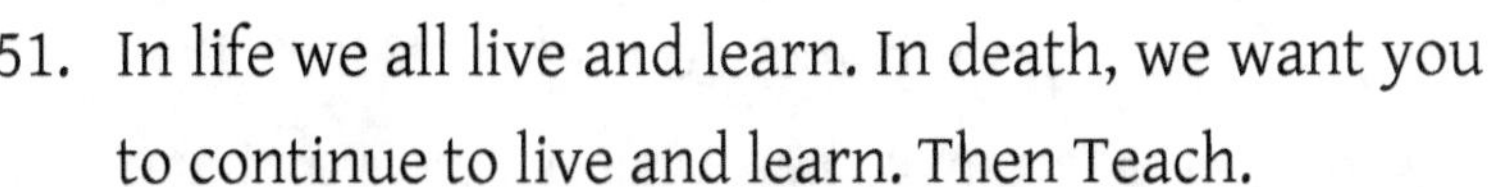

51. In life we all live and learn. In death, we want you to continue to live and learn. Then Teach.

52. No one today walks a path of perfectness, so try not to point fingers at anyone.

53. If your timing is wrong, you have to wonder; will it Ever be Right?

54. People say, if Loving you is wrong, I don't want to be right. I say that, you can Never be wrong, if you are in Love.

55. I don't cater to no one. You'd better learn how to do this and learn how to do that.

56. You came in and changed my world, so I owe you.

57. WE need to do what we need to do.

58. Why ask a question that you can answer yourself?

59. I am not trying to keep up with the Jones's because I am a Jones.

60. If everyone is wrong, no one can be right.

61. A monster could be lurking under your bed whispering in your ear, but there can be an Angel over your head telling you not to fear.

62. If you are not in it to win it, you shouldn't be in it at all.

63. If you really want something good out of life, you have to put up with a lot of grief and strife.

64. One thing about life is you don't understand it, until it beats you up.

65. One question about our life is will we Ever be Free?

66. You can love the sunshine, but you have to sometimes appreciate the Rains.

67. You can't color a fault or touch an emotion?

68. Does it take a fool to learn?

69. Doors are wide open for you and me in the game of life.

70. If we don't change things, things will never change.

71. Truth and Justice are always the ways of the Lord Thy God.

72. Even a short gain is making progress.

73. If you want to chase your dreams, make sure you never stop.

74. The best part of waking up is having loved ones in your life.

75. Why would you want to just get your head out from under a foot, instead of getting your whole body out?

76. You should always, do your best to win, but know how to lose.

77. Believe in yourself and don't worry about what others think about you.

78. Will there Ever be an end of an end?

79. Every decision that you make in your life effects your next decision.

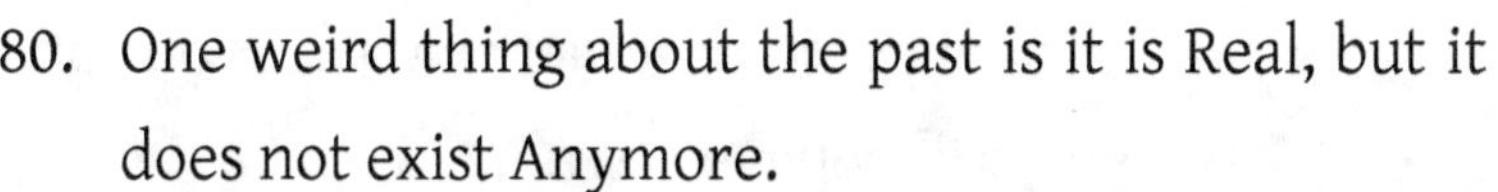

80. One weird thing about the past is it is Real, but it does not exist Anymore.

81. Whether you Win or Lose, you should Learn.

82. The good doesn't always win, but the bad never truly wins.

83. If age is nothing but a number, why is that number always changing?

84. If you sin against Life, you will pay dearly in the end.

85. We All should let the laughter of a child remind us who we used to be.

86. Some days I may seem to be weak, but I refuse to cry.

87. May All the advice that you receive in life be useful.

88. In my professional opinion, the customer is not Always right. But to keep your business intact, you have to treat them like they are always right.

89. When good men and women do nothing about Evil that is when Evil will run amuck.

90. Sometimes what is ordinary for you is perfect for me.

91. Integris is the uprightness of being honest and holding oneself to having strong moral principles to moral and ethical standards.

92. If you believe in me, I should believe in you.

93. Faith is believing in something that you can't see, but you still believe is true.

94. If you want me, you can have me, if you Really believe in me.

95. More is better when it is right and when it is good.

96. You can Never go back to a place that you have Never been.

97. One dream can die and from that dream a whole other dream can be born.

98. Our life is like math, once you put the equation in the proper order of operation, you can only come to the truth.

99. Some people's opinions aren't Always valued.

100. If you live for me, I will die for you.

www.ingramcontent.com/pod-product-compliance
Lightning Source LLC
Chambersburg PA
CBHW071202300726
48975CB00004B/1254